鲁比·布里奇斯

Heroes and Role Models | Non-Fiction Series

Copyright © 2022 by Level Learning, INC. and Washington Yu Ying PCS™
Original and Edited Text Copyright © 2022 by Washington Yu Ying PCS™

All rights reserved. No part of this book in whole or part may be reproduced without written permission from the publisher.

Published by Level Learning, INC.

Content Contributors:
Washington Yu Ying PCS™
Level Learning - Ya-Ching Chang

Illustrations by: Josh Taira

Leveling classification based on Level Learning standard. For full description, visit www.levellearning.com

ISBN 978-1-64040-044-3
Traditional Chinese Edition

About Level Learning:

Level Learning provides a literacy focused curriculum specifically designed for K-12 Chinese as a Second Language classrooms. Our program offers 20 levels of specific and detailed objectives, leveled texts and passages, mastery-based online assessment, and analytics to enable data-driven instruction. Level Learning reading curriculum for both literature and informational text emphasize grammar and comprehension skills to help teachers develop confident and independent Chinese language readers. The non-fiction series of books are specifically designed to support our informational text course based on multiple national standards. To learn more about our entire offering, visit www.levellearning.com.

About Washington Yu Ying PCS™:

Washington Yu Ying PCS is a Mandarin English dual language immersion International Baccalaureate (IB) World school. Yu Ying's mission is to inspire and prepare young people to create a better world by challenging them to reach their full potential in a nurturing Chinese/English educational environment. Yu Ying's comprehensive IB, dual immersion curriculum equips students with global competencies for success in the real world. As a leader in immersion education, Yu Ying is determined to advance Chinese language programs and global citizenry education by helping other schools create and strengthen their Chinese programs. For more information, email: products@washingtonyuying.org

在1950年到1970年期間，許多美國人覺得白人和非洲裔是不一樣的。白人和非洲裔在不同的學校讀書；在不同的餐館吃飯；在不同的地方居住。這種現象被稱為「種族隔離」。

當時的美國政府想做一些改變。政府想讓白人和非洲裔生活在同樣的環境裡。但是，住在美國南方的許多白人並不喜歡這個改變。

在1960年，有一個叫魯比的非洲裔女孩到白人的學校上學。這件事受到許多人的反對，因為人們不希望非洲裔出現在白人的學校裡。許多父母也不希望他們的孩子和非洲裔一起上學。

魯比上學的第一天，有一群人聚集在學校外面抗議。這些人不停地喊叫著，叫魯比趕快離開這所學校。為了保護魯比，警察只好陪著她一起進入學校。但是魯比一點也不害怕，因為她相信這是一所很好的學校。

進入學校後，魯比卻被叫到校長室，因為有許多老師和學生不想和魯比一起上課。後來，終於有一位老師願意給魯比上課了。雖然教室裡只有她和老師兩個人，魯比還是很認真地聽課。

剛開始去學校的這幾天，魯比知道自己不受歡迎，但是她還是鼓起勇氣去學校。就這樣一天又一天，魯比每天都去上學。第二年，魯比慢慢地交到了一些朋友，其他人也願意和她一起上課了。老師和學生慢慢地看到魯比和大家一樣的地方，而不再只關注她的膚色了。

後來，越來越多的人知道了魯比的故事。有人把她的故事拍成影片，也有人把她的故事寫成書。現在，大家相信「種族融合」，而不再是「種族隔離」了。現在，不只是白人和非洲裔，其他很多不同種族、不同膚色的人也都平等地生活在一起了。

Glossary

	Pinyin	English Definition
非洲裔	fēi zhōu yì	African descent
一樣	yí yàng	same
餐館	cān guǎn	restaurant
居住	jū zhù	to live
現象	xiàn xiàng	phenomenon
種族隔離	zhǒng zú gé lí	racial segregation
政府	zhèng fǔ	government
改變	gǎi biàn	change
同樣	tóng yàng	the same
環境	huán jìng	surrounding
受到	shòu dào	receive
反對	fǎn duì	against, disagreement
出現	chū xiàn	to appear
上學	shàng xué	to go to school
聚集	jù jí	to gather

	Pinyin	English Definition
抗議	kàng yì	to protest
喊叫	hǎn jiào	to yell, to scream
趕快	gǎn kuài	hurry up
離開	lí kāi	to leave
保護	bǎo hù	to protect
陪	péi	to accompany
害怕	hài pà	afraid
相信	xiāng xìn	to believe
校長室	xiào zhǎng shì	Principal's office
願意	yuàn yì	willing
教室	jiào shì	classroom
認真	rèn zhēn	serious
歡迎	huān yíng	welcome
鼓起	gǔ qǐ	to muster
勇氣	yǒng qì	courage

	Pinyin	English Definition
關注	guān zhù	to pay attention
膚色	fū sè	skin color
越來越多	yuè lái yuè duō	more and more
影片	yǐng piān	movie
種族融合	zhǒng zú róng hé	racial integration

www.ingramcontent.com/pod-product-compliance
Lightning Source LLC
Chambersburg PA
CBHW041225070526
44584CB00001B/99